**A Grammar of Spoken English
Exercises 2: Communication**

D1654971

John Eastwood · Ronald Mackin

A Grammar of Spoken English

Exercises 2: Communication

Cornelsen & Oxford University Press

Verfasser   John Eastwood, M. A., Street/Somerset
Ronald Mackin, M. A., Colchester/Essex

Redaktion   Michael Freyer

Zeichnungen   Hewett Street Studios, London

Die Übungen in diesem Band sind "A Grammar of Spoken English" *(GSE)* von R. Mackin und J. Eastwood zugeordnet. Sie korrespondieren mit den Kapiteln 32–36 der Grammatik und üben die dort beschriebenen kommunikativen Funktionen. Jede Übung ist sowohl durchlaufend numeriert als auch durch den entsprechenden Abschnitt in der Grammatik gekennzeichnet. Es besteht daher immer die Möglichkeit, auf die Grammatik zurückzugreifen.
Der jedem Übungsbuch beiliegende Schlüssel *(Key)* bietet die Lösung zu allen Übungen.

1. Auflage 1984

Bestellnummer 5518

© Cornelsen & Oxford University Press GmbH, Berlin 1984

Alle Rechte vorbehalten

Die Vervielfältigung und Übertragung, auch einzelner Textabschnitte, Bilder oder Zeichnungen, ist – mit Ausnahme der Vervielfältigung zum persönlichen und eigenen Gebrauch gemäß §§ 53, 54 URG – ohne schriftliche Zustimmung des Verlages nicht zulässig. Das gilt sowohl für die Vervielfältigung durch Fotokopie oder irgendein anderes Verfahren als auch für die Übertragung auf Filme, Bänder, Platten, Arbeitstransparente oder andere Medien.

Satz/Druck Saladruck Steinkopf & Sohn, Berlin

Repros ORT Kirchner & Graser, Berlin

Weiterverarbeitung Fritzsche/Ludwig, Berlin

ISBN 3-8109-0551-8

Vertrieb Cornelsen-Velhagen & Klasing Verlagsgesellschaft, Bielefeld

Contents

Starting and finishing a conversation *(GSE 32)* 7
Statements and opinions *(GSE 33)* 12
Telling and asking people to do things *(GSE 34)* 21
Feelings *(GSE 35)* 38
Right and wrong *(GSE 36)* 47
General Communication *(GSE 32–36)* 51
Index 62

Starting and finishing a conversation

Exercise 1

32.2 Introductions

These sentences were all spoken at a party last Saturday. Write down the five sentences that were used to introduce people.

Here's Philip, look.
This is my sister Lucy.
Hi, Alan.
Regards to Dave.
Philip, meet Sarah.

Hello, Julia.
Let me introduce you to Mr Jones.
Kate, I'd like you to meet my mother.
How are you, Gary?
Alan, have you met Kate?

Exercise 2

32.4 On the telephone

Judy is making a phone call. Kevin answers the phone.

Write the dialogue in the correct order.

Judy: Hello. Is that Somerton 74232?
Judy: Oh, dear. Well, can you ask him to ring me, please?
Judy: Thanks, Kevin. Bye!
Judy: This is Judy. Is Alex there, please?

Kevin: Bye!
Kevin: Hello?
Kevin: Oh, hello, Judy. No, I'm afraid he isn't. He won't be back until this evening.
Kevin: Yes, OK. I'll do that.
Kevin: Yes, it is. Who's speaking, please?

Begin like this:

Kevin: Hello?
Judy: Hello. ...

Exercise 3

32.3 + 32.5 Saying hello to someone you know

Two people meet in the street. They know each other quite well, but they haven't met for some time. Here are some of the things they might say.

Hello.
Hi.

Hi. How's life?
Hello. How are you?

Very well, thank you. And how are you?
Fine, thanks. And you?

OK, thanks.
Not too bad, thank you.

I'm afraid I have to go. My bus leaves in two minutes.
I must dash. I'm running for a bus.

That's all right. Goodbye.
OK. So long!

See you! Cheerio!
Goodbye.

Choose the less formal of each pair of sentences and write the sentences out to make an informal conversation. Begin like this:

Hi.
Hi. How's life?
...

Then use the other sentences to write a more formal conversation.

Exercise 4

32.7 Good wishes

What might you say in these situations? Write the expressions with the correct numbers.

1 on January 1st	Good luck.
2 when it's someone's birthday	Have a good trip.
3 to someone who is going to take an exam	Happy New Year!
4 to someone who is moving away to start a new life	Many happy returns!
	Enjoy yourself.
5 to someone who is going to a party	All the best.
6 to someone who is going on a journey	

Exercise 5
32.8 Compliments
Compliment people on their clothes.

Examples
sweater/super
That's a super sweater.

stockings/nice
Those are nice stockings

1 coat/smart
2 jeans/nice
3 boots/super
4 dress/lovely
5 trousers/smart
6 shirt/very nice

Exercise 6

32 Starting and finishing a conversation
Find the correct reply.

Example
Hi! – Hi!

1 Hi!	Bye!
2 How do you do?	Hi!
3 How are you?	How do you do?
4 See you.	I'm glad you enjoyed it.
5 My grandmother has just died.	Very well, thank you.
6 That was a very nice meal.	Oh, I'm sorry.

10 Starting and finishing a conversation

Exercise 7

32 Starting and finishing a conversation

Which of these expressions belongs to which picture?

Cheers! / Good afternoon. / Have a good time. / How do you do? / Never mind. / Well done!

Write the expressions with the correct numbers.

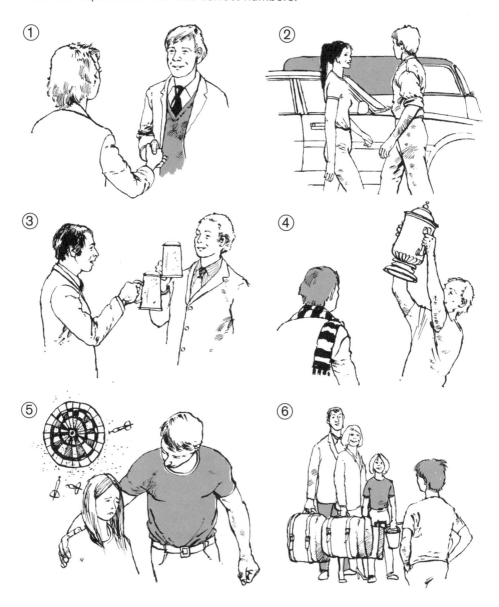

Exercise 8

32 Starting and finishing a conversation

What might you say in these situations? Write the expressions with the correct number.

1	to say goodbye to a friend	Who's speaking?
2	at the end of a letter	Excuse me.
3	when someone rings you up	How are you?
4	when you speak to a stranger in the street	Yours sincerely.
5	when someone has lost a game	Cheerio!
6	when you meet a friend	Bad luck.

Statements and opinions

Exercise 9

33.1 Agreeing with a statement
Agree with the statements.

Examples
It's a lovely day.
Yes, it is.

These posters look great.
Yes, they do.

1 The film was terrific.
2 It'll be your birthday soon.
3 Ron Fowler played well in the match last night.
4 I'm early.
5 The days are getting shorter.
6 There's plenty of time.
7 The door needs oiling.
8 You're tired.

Exercise 10

33.1 Correcting a statement
Correct the statements.

Examples
The match is on Tuesday. *(Wednesday)*
No, it isn't. It's on Wednesday.

Julia comes from Devon. *(Cornwall)*
No, she doesn't. She comes from Cornwall.

1 The banks close at three. *(half past three)*
2 Mr Simpson plays basketball. *(volley-ball)*
3 You'll be fifteen next year. *(sixteen)*
4 The Browns have gone to Greece. *(Yugoslavia)*
5 The last disco was two weeks ago. *(three weeks ago)*
6 I can park for an hour here. *(half an hour)*
7 The pub opposite the church is the Red Lion. *(the Dog and Duck)*
8 You gave me a pound note. *(a five-pound note)*

Exercise 11

33.2 Asking the meaning of a word

Klaus is staying in England with his friend Andrew. Klaus often asks Andrew the meaning of English words.

Write Klaus's questions.

Example

Klaus: What does 'congested' mean?
Andrew: 'Congested' means 'crowded', 'full of people and traffic'.

1 *Klaus:*   ...
   Andrew: 'Commence'? It means 'to begin'.

2 *Klaus:*   ...
   Andrew: 'Seldom' means 'not very often'.

3 *Klaus:*   ...
   Andrew: A 'bachelor' is an unmarried man.

4 *Klaus:*   ...
   Andrew: 'Assist' means to 'help'.

5 *Klaus:*   ...
   Andrew: Well, if you 'observe' something, you watch it carefully.

6 *Klaus:*   ...
   Andrew: 'Enormous'? It means 'very big'.

7 *Klaus:*   ...
   Andrew: 'Identical' means 'exactly the same'.

8 *Klaus:*   ...
   Andrew: 'Perilous' means the same as 'dangerous'.

Exercise 12

33.2 Asking for a word

The pupils are asking the teacher to tell them words that they don't know. Write the pupils' questions.

Examples

(He sells meat.)
Pupil: What's the word for someone who sells meat?
Teacher: That's a 'butcher'.

(You carry food on it.)
Pupil: What's the word for something you carry food on?
Teacher: We call it a 'tray'.

1. *(He/She travels on a bus or train.)*
   Pupil: ...
   Teacher: You mean a 'passenger'.

2. *(You cut paper with it.)*
   Pupil: ...
   Teacher: We say 'a pair of scissors'.

3. *(You hang clothes in it.)*
   Pupil: ...
   Teacher: That's a 'wardrobe'.

4. *(He/She repairs cars.)*
   Pupil: ...
   Teacher: A 'mechanic'.

5. *(He/She paints pictures.)*
   Pupil: ...
   Teacher: You mean an 'artist'.

6. *(You hold it when you open a door.)*
   Pupil: ...
   Teacher: You mean a 'handle'.

7. *(You carry an injured person on it.)*
   Pupil: ...
   Teacher: That's a 'stretcher'.

8. *(He/She sells fruit and vegetables.)*
   Pupil: ...
   Teacher: We say a 'greengrocer'.

Exercise 13

33.3 Asking for an explanation

Add a sentence with **I don't understand ...** to ask for an explanation.

Example

What's the problem? I don't understand what the problem is.

1 Why do I have to pay?
2 What are you worrying about?
3 How did the accident happen?
4 What am I supposed to do?
5 How did you find out?
6 Why can't I sit in this seat?
7 Where did we go wrong?
8 What does this paragraph mean?

Exercise 14

33.4 Being sure and unsure

Read the sentences and decide how sure the speaker is. Write **a** for sure, **b** for less sure and **c** for unsure. If you think the speaker in the first sentence isn't very sure about Mr Parsons being out, then write 1 **b)**. After your answer write the word or words that tell you how sure the speaker is, e g 1 **b) believe.**

1 I believe Mr Parsons is out at the moment.
2 I don't know what the time is.
3 I doubt if we can afford to buy new furniture.
4 I expect you're right.
5 I know they're on holiday this week.
6 I may see Laura tomorrow.
7 I'm certain I paid the bill.
8 I'm not sure where Castle Street is.
9 I'm sure I sent the Davidsons a Christmas card.
10 I should think we've time for a cup of coffee.
11 I've no idea what Brian's doing these days.
12 Perhaps they missed the train.
13 There must be something wrong with the heater.
14 We might be able to get a meal at the pub.
15 You definitely said Thursday.

Exercise 15

33.4 Being sure and unsure

Write sentences showing that you are sure (v), less sure (?) or unsure (??). Use **I'm sure ...**, **I think ...** and **I don't know. ...**

Examples

The supermarket's open today. *(v)*
I'm sure the supermarket's open today.

I've been here before. *(?)*
I think I've been here before.

Did England win? *(??)*
I don't know if England won.

1. The film is at half past seven. *(?)*
2. When does the last bus go? *(??)*
3. I told you about the meeting. *(v)*
4. The school's got a computer. *(?)*
5. This is the right way. *(v)*
6. Does Vicky play the piano? *(??)*
7. There's a phone box outside the pub. *(?)*
8. You'll like Cornwall. *(v)*
9. I put the keys in the drawer. *(v)*
10. Has Kevin got a ticket? *(??)*
11. I locked the back door. *(?)*
12. Why didn't Nicholas come and see us? *(??)*

Exercise 16

33.5 Asking for an opinion

Add a sentence with **Are you in favour of ...?** to ask someone's opinion.

Example

Should taxes be increased? Are you in favour of increasing taxes?

1. Should the factory be closed?
2. Ought prices to be frozen?
3. Do you think a by-pass should be built?
4. Ought cars to be kept out of cities?
5. Do you think alcohol ought to be banned?
6. Should more money be spent on nuclear bombs?

Exercise 17

33.5 Opinions

James and Sarah are talking about a hotel that has just been built in the town where they live.

Write the dialogue in the correct order. Then look at each sentence and say if the speaker is asking for an opinion, giving an opinion, agreeing or disagreeing. (Sometimes the speaker does more than one of these things.)

James: Oh, I wouldn't say that. I think it looks all right.
James: But on the other hand they bring money with them.
James: What do you think about the new hotel, Sarah?
James: But don't you think they'll attract more tourists? Tourism is a good thing for the town.
Sarah: I don't agree. It's far too big. In my opinion we don't need all these hotel beds, anyway.
Sarah: Exactly. And money is the only reason for building an ugly thing like that.
Sarah: Do you really think so? As far as I can see, tourists are a nuisance.
Sarah: Personally, I think it's awful. It spoils the whole street.

Exercise 18

33.6 Predictions

Only five of these sentences are predictions. Write down the five predictions.

I expect Paul's out on his bike.
Bill Wilkins is bound to be the next Prime Minister.
I expect Oxford will win the boat race again.
I'll help you with these bags.
Your father's so fit, I'm sure he'll live to be a hundred.
I'll tidy my room tomorrow, I promise.
There'll be no oil left at all in thirty years' time.
I'm sure I saw Nicola in the market yesterday.
I think it's going to rain.
We're going to Brighton in August.

Exercise 19

33.6 Predictions

Rewrite the predictions using **be sure to.**

Example

I'm sure Philip will forget the tickets.
Philip is sure to forget the tickets.

1. I'm sure Karen will do well in her exams.
2. I'm sure the train is going to be late.
3. I'm sure Tony will get the job.
4. I'm sure United are going to lose.
5. I'm sure it's going to snow.
6. I'm sure this car is going to fall to pieces soon.

Exercise 20

33.7 Imagining situations

Neil Dawson is a writer of science fiction stories. Here are some of his ideas for stories.

> Computers rule the world.
> Napoleon won the Battle of Waterloo.
> The Americans lost the war of Independence.
> There's a war in space.
> Martians control our thoughts.
> Britain sinks into the sea.
> The dinosaurs didn't die out.
> Trees learn to walk.
> A group of terrorists capture the US President.

Write sentences with **Supposing** .... Use the past tense for things that Neil imagines might happen in the future; use the past perfect tense for things that could have happened in the past.

Examples

Supposing computers ruled the world.
Supposing Napoleon had won the Battle of Waterloo.

Exercise 21

33 Statements and opinions

Find the correct reply.

1	I just don't see why we can't leave now.	As far as I'm concerned, it's a waste of money.
2	I think schoolchildren should wear a uniform.	It's ten past actually.
3	It's five past two now.	It's a kind of fish.
4	It was cold yesterday.	I don't agree.
5	What do you think about sending people into space?	Well, the thing is we haven't got a driver.
6	What's a 'herring'?	Yes, it was.

Example

I just don't see why we can't leave now. – Well, the thing is we haven't got a driver.

Exercise 22

33 Statements and opinions

How might you use the phrases and sentences on the right? Write each of the numbers 1–6 with the correct phrase or sentence.

1	to agree with an opinion	I bet...
2	to disagree with an opinion	I don't get you.
3	when you are imagining a situation	I see.
4	when you don't understand what a friend says to you	I wouldn't say that.
		Quite.
5	to make a prediction	What if ...
6	to say that you understand	

Exercise 23

33 Statements and opinions

Write six sensible sentences.

1 Could you explain 2 In my opinion, 3 Just imagine if 4 I'm sure 5 What do you call it 6 What's the meaning	when lessons stop for twenty minutes? how this toaster works? the government should do something about it. the Americans will win lots of medals. of this word here? we had lots of money.

Telling and asking people to do things

Exercise 24

34.1, 34.11 + 34.12   Orders, offers and invitations

Read these sentences carefully and write down the five sentences which are most likely to be orders.

Come and stay with us for a day or two.
Come here.
Don't move!
Have some coffee.
Help yourself to potatoes.
Put the books on my desk.
Show me your homework.
Sit down, won't you?
Take this medicine.
Use my bike if you like.

Exercise 25

34.1   Orders

Colin isn't doing very well at school. His class teacher, Mrs Andrews, is having a talk with him. Write her sentences using this table.

You	must mustn't	take more care with your work. do your homework. forget to do it. dream all day. listen in class. miss classes. be late for school. try harder.

Exercise 26

34.1 + 33.4 Orders and being sure

Read these sentences carefully and write down the four sentences which are orders.

You must be home before eleven o'clock.
You must be hot in that coat.
You must be tired after your walk.
You must fill in the form.
You must have some idea where you left your pen.
You must pay this bill by April 30th.
You must take the pills before meals.
You must think I'm stupid.

Exercise 27

34.1 Orders

The road signs tell you what to do and what not to do. Write what the signs say. Use these words and expressions: **cycle, go slow, go straight ahead, keep left, look left, overtake, park, stop, turn left, turn right.**

Examples

You're to stop.
You're not to turn left.

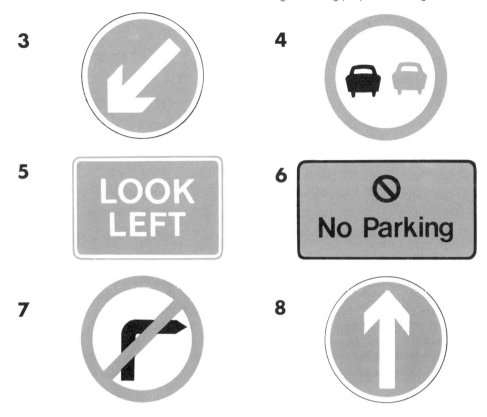

Exercise 28

34.2 Requests

Ask someone to do the following things. Use the words in brackets.

Examples

pass you the milk *(will)*
Will you pass me the milk, please?

open the window *(would mind)*
Would you mind opening the window, please?

1 help you *(could)*
2 make some coffee *(would like)*
3 write down his/her name and address *(can)*
4 go to the supermarket for you *(would mind)*
5 keep a seat for you *(would)*
6 hold your bag for a moment *(will)*
7 give you some information *(could)*
8 tidy up a bit *(would like)*

24 Telling and asking people to do things

Exercise 29

34.3 Intentions

What do people say in these situations? Use the words in brackets.

Examples

Jonathan doesn't like his job. It's his intention to look for a new one. *(decide)*
Jonathan: I've decided to look for a new job.

Mr und Mrs Exton usually stay at home at Christmas but this year it's their intention to go away, although they're still unsure about it. *(might)*
Mr and Mrs Exton: We might go away at Christmas.

1 Claire needs a holiday. It's her intention to take one in July. *(plan)*
2 Mr and Mrs Young haven't seen their daughter in Canada for a long time. It's their intention to visit her, although they're still unsure about it. *(think)*
3 Anthony is good at tennis. There's a tennis competition next week, and it's his intention to take part in it. *(going to)*
4 Michael is tired. His intention is to go to bed early. *(intend)*
5 Paul hasn't spoken to his girl-friend for a few days. It's his intention to ring her later, although he isn't sure about it. *(might)*
6 Elizabeth is interested in computers. It's her intention to buy one. *(decide)*
7 Anne doesn't use her bike now. It's her intention to sell it, although she isn't sure about it. *(think)*
8 Mr and Mrs Dale's house is too big for them now. It's their intention to move to a smaller one. *(going to)*

Exercise 30

34.4 Suggestions

Suggest that you and your friend do the following things. Use the words in brackets.

Example

have a party *(how about)*
How about having a party?

1 listen to the news *(shall)*
2 get a taxi *(why not)*
3 have some lunch *(what about)*
4 take a picnic *(could)*
5 buy some postcards *(how about)*
6 go out somewhere *(why don't)*
7 play some records *(shall)*
8 sit on the wall *(let's)*

Exercise 31

34.4 Suggestions

Write the dialogue with the correct expressions.

Martin:	How about / How would it be / What with	a game of tennis?		

Alex:	I think it's a bit hot for me,	actually. / instead. / on the other hand.		

Martin:	Do we / Shall we / Will we	play chess	better, / instead, / rather,	then?

Alex:	Exactly. / Fine, thanks. / Good idea.	Let's / Suggest / Want	sit out in the garden,	are we? / shall we? / will we?

Martin:	Indeed. / OK. / Quite.	How can't we / What about / Why don't we	sit under the tree?	

Alex:	No, why not? / Yes, let's do that. / Yes, we do.			

Exercise 32

34.5 Advice

These people need advice. What do they say? Write sentences with **What should I/we do about...?**

Example

The Atkinsons' heating isn't working, and they don't know what's wrong with it.

Mr and Mrs Atkinson: What should we do about the heating?

1 Mary is going to Germany. She'll need money while she's there, but she doesn't want to carry a lot with her all the time.
2 Mr and Mrs Pritchard have bought tickets for a concert, but they can't go now because their daughter is ill. The tickets were quite expensive.
3 Terry is going to a party, but it's four miles away, and he hasn't got transport.
4 The Prices are booking a holiday, but their dog Brandy can't go with them because pets aren't allowed at the place they're going to.
5 Alan is travelling by train, but he's got too much luggage to carry.

Exercise 33

34.5 Advice

Reply to these people. Give advice using **had better**. Use these words: **clean it up, get it repaired, have a rest, hurry, not smoke, shut the window, wash them.**

Example

David: These socks are dirty.
You: You'd better wash them, then.

1 *Jessica:* I'm late for the meeting.
2 *Neil:* I've spilt milk all over the floor.
3 *Peter:* I'm cold.
4 *Louise:* The television isn't working.
5 *Mr Davis:* I've been digging the garden all afternoon, and I'm tired.
6 *Simon:* It says 'No Smoking' over there.

Exercise 34

34.5 Advice

Advise people to do the following things. Use the words in brackets.

Examples

phone the police   *(should)*
I think you should phone the police.

not do anything in a hurry   *(advise)*
I'd advise you not to do anything in a hurry.

1. go to hospital   *(ought)*
2. find a flat   *(best thing)*
3. not go out in this weather   *(if I were you)*
4. complain   *(should)*
5. find out more information   *(if you ask me)*
6. book your ticket now   *(advise)*
7. think it over for a day or two   *(best thing)*
8. not visit the Lake District in summer   *(if you take my advice)*

Exercise 35

34.6 Warnings

Combine each pair of sentences using **If..., ...will/might....**

Examples

Look after that money. You might lose it.
If you don't look after that money, you might lose it.

Don't touch the iron. You'll burn yourself.
If you touch the iron, you'll burn yourself.

1. Don't sit on that chair. You'll get wet paint on your clothes.
2. Lock your bike. It might get stolen.
3. Be careful. You might fall.
4. Don't try to lift that stone. You'll hurt yourself.
5. Hurry up. We might miss the bus.
6. Don't open the oven door. You'll spoil the cake.
7. Don't leave those pills on the table. The baby might get them.
8. Take it easy. You'll make yourself ill.

Exercise 36

34.7 Threats

Rewrite the threats using an imperative and **or.**

Examples

If you don't get out of here, I'll throw you out.
Get out of here or I'll throw you out!

If you come in here, I'll scream.
Don't come in here or I'll scream!

1. If you don't go away, I'll get my dogs.
2. If you make a sound, I'll hit you.
3. If you don't behave yourself, I'll never speak to you again.
4. If you don't let go, I'll tell the teacher.
5. If you touch me, you'll be sorry.
6. If you don't give me the money, I'll call the police.
7. If you don't move out of my way, I'll knock you over.
8. If you come round here again, we'll teach you a lesson.

Exercise 37

34.8 Insisting

Report what people insisted on.

Example

Philip: I really must count the money.
Philip insisted on counting the money.

1. *Mrs Bray:* I'm sorry to insist, but I must see the manager.
2. *Bob and Sarah:* We really must leave early.
3. *Mr Fletcher:* It's absolutely essential I know the truth.
4. *Kate:* I really must show you my holiday photos.
5. *Students:* We don't have enough time. We insist on having more.
6. *Mr Booker:* I'm sorry to insist, but we must change the date of the sports day.

Exercise 38

34.9 Persuading

Write the dialogue with the correct expressions.

| Janet: | Don't we want / Why don't you / Won't you better | come jogging with us, Simon? |

Simon: No, thanks.

| Janet: | But please! / Do so. / Why not? | Jogging's good for you. |

Simon: I hate jogging.

| Janet: | Oh, | come on, / how about, / watch out, | Simon. It's fun. |

| Judy: | But yes. / Go on. / Let's. | You'll like it. |

| Janet: | Look, / Please, / Think, | you really ought to keep fit, Simon. |

Simon: I **am** fit. I'm not overweight.

Judy: You soon will be if you sit in a chair all day.

| | If you ask me, / Let me say / You really must | take a little exercise, you know. |

Telling and asking people to do things

| Simon: | All right, then.
Mind,
That's it. | I might try it some time. |

Exercise 39

34.10 Promises

Write what people say when they make promises.

Example

Susan hasn't tidied her room. She promises her mother she'll do it at the weekend.

Susan: I'll tidy my room at the weekend, I promise.

1 Lucy often comes home late. She promises her parents she'll come home early tonight.
2 Robert has been in trouble. He promises his teacher he'll stay out of trouble in future.
3 Ian didn't work very hard last term. He promises his parents he'll work harder next term.
4 Joanne hasn't written her essay. She promises her English teacher she'll do it tomorrow.
5 Colin forgot to post the letters for his mother. He promises her he'll do it before half past five.
6 Sadie borrowed a record of Kevin's some time ago. She promises to give him it back tomorrow.

Exercise 40

34.10 + 34.7 Promises and threats

Read these sentences carefully and write down the four sentences which are promises.

I'll break every bone in your body.
I'll cause plenty of trouble for you.
I'll do my best for you.
I'll see everything is OK.
I'll send you a postcard.
I'll use this gun.
You'll have the cheque by the end of the week.
You'll wish you'd never come here.

Exercise 41

34.11 Offering to help

Offer to help. Use the words in brackets.

Examples

Judy has just cooked a meal for you, but she's too tired to wash up. *(Would you like ...)*
Would you like me to wash up?

Lucy can't move the table on her own. She needs someone to help her move it. *(I'll ...)*
I'll help you move it.

1 Stephen has lost a tennis ball and can't find it. He needs someone to help him look for it. *(Let me ...)*
2 David can't carry the ladder on his own. He needs someone to help him carry it. *(Can I ...)*
3 Now David is going to climb the ladder, but he needs someone to hold it for him. *(I'll ...)*
4 Angela's trying to open a jar, but she can't open it. *(Shall I ...)*
5 Mrs Phillips has got a letter, but she can't read it very well. She needs someone to read it to her. *(Would you like ...)*
6 Alan has to do the shopping, but he's in a bit of a hurry. Offer to do it for him. *(Shall I ...)*
7 Carl has got a letter to post. You are on your way to the post office. *(Can I ...)*
8 You plan to go to the theatre with a friend. One of you will have to get the tickets. *(Would you like ...)*
9 Your friend wants to buy a record but hasn't got any money. Offer to lend your friend some money. *(I'll ...)*
10 Pauline's car won't start. She needs someone to give her a push. *(Let me ...)*

Exercise 42

34.11 Offering food or drink

Complete these offers of food and drink. Use **have** or **like** and **a/an** or **some.**

1 Will ... apple?
2 Would ... wine?
3 Do ... beans.
4 Would ... sweet?
5 Won't ... sandwich?
6 Will ... carrots?
7 Would ... chocolate biscuit?
8 Do ... cheese.
9 Would ... fruit?
10 Do ... more coffee.

Telling and asking people to do things

Exercise 43

34.11 Offering and asking permission

Five of these sentences are offers and five are requests for permission. Write down the five sentences which are offers.

Can I borrow this book?
Can we do anything to help?
Can I pass you a biscuit?
Can we walk on the grass?
Can I take you anywhere in the car?
Can we sit here, please?
Can I use your pen?
Can we give you a bed for the night?
Can I do that for you?
Can I see the letter?

Exercise 44

34.12 Invitations

Sarah invites Kevin to a disco. Kevin can't go, but he invites Sarah to one later.

Write the dialogue in the correct order.

Kevin: Oh, well, I'm afraid I can't. I'm visiting my cousin in London next weekend.
Kevin: Yes, it is. But I expect I'll be having a disco too on my birthday. How about coming to mine?
Kevin: Yes, that'd be great.
Kevin: Yes, I would. When is it?
Sarah: It's next Saturday.
Sarah: Oh, that's a pity.
Sarah: Would you like to come to a disco, Kevin? Louise and I are having a disco for our birthdays.
Sarah: Yes, fine. Thanks. I'll look forward to that.

Exercise 45

34.12 Refusing an invitation

Refuse invitations using the following excuses. Begin **That's very kind of you, but ...** or **I'd love to, but ...** .

Example

Neil: Would you like to stay at our house for the afternoon?
You have to go to the dentist. *(kind)*

That's very kind of you, but I have to go to the dentist.

1 *Tony:* Do you want to come to my party on Saturday?
  You'll be away on holiday. *(love)*
2 *Mrs Davis:* Would you like to have dinner with us?
  You ought to do some studying for your exam. *(kind)*
3 *Judy:* Won't you come for a swim?
  You aren't feeling very well. *(love)*
4 *Martin:* How about coming round to us this evening?
  You've agreed to babysit for someone. *(love)*
5 *Laura:* Do come and see us tomorrow.
  You've got some friends staying with you. *(kind)*
6 *Mr Price:* Would you like a lift to London on Thursday?
  There's an important meeting you have to go to on that day. *(kind)*

Exercise 46

34.12 + 34.2 Invitations and requests

Five of these sentences are invitations and five are requests. Write down the five sentences which are invitations.

Would you like to type this letter?
Would you like to make the coffee?
Would you like to come for coffee?
Would you like to give us some help?
Would you like to go for a walk with us?
Would you like to come to a concert?
Would you like to tidy things up a bit?
Would you like to spend the night here?
Would you like to have a meal with us?
Would you like to fill in this form?

34 Telling and asking people to do things

Exercise 47

34.13 Thanks

Say how you would thank people. Use the best of these four phrases in each situation.

Thanks.
Thanks a lot.
Thank you.
Thank you very much.

1 a friend who translates a letter into English for you
2 a teacher who hands you your English book
3 a friend who gives you a sweet
4 an English friend who lends you his bicycle during your stay in England
5 a policeman who has given you very detailed directions how to find a street you are looking for
6 a shop assistant who gives you your change
7 a shop assistant who runs after you with a bag you left behind in the shop
8 a friend who picks up a pen you have dropped on the floor

Exercise 48

34 Telling and asking people to do things

Find the correct reply.

Example

Could you help us? – Yes, of course.

1 Could you help us?	I can manage, thank you.
2 Do come and visit us.	It's a pleasure.
3 Let me help.	That would be lovely. Thank you.
4 Shall we go now?	Yes, of course.
5 Thank you very much.	Yes, please.
6 Would you like a biscuit?	Yes, why not?

Exercise 49

34 Telling and asking people to do things

How might you use the following phrases? Write each of the numbers 1–8 with the correct phrase.

1	to express an intention	How about …?
2	to give an order	If you ask me, …
3	to give advice	I'm going to …
4	to insist on something	It's absolutely essential …
5	to make a request	Let me …
6	to make a suggestion	That's very kind of you, but …
7	to offer help	Would you mind …?
8	to refuse an invitation	You're to …

Exercise 50

34 Telling and asking people to do things

Which of these expressions belongs to which picture?

Be careful./Excuse me./Look out!/No, thank you./Pardon?/Thank you.

Exercise 51

34 Telling and asking people to do things

What might you say in these situations? Write the expressions with the correct numbers.

1	thanking someone	Allow me.
2	to agree with a suggestion	Don't mention it.
3	to ask for advice	Good idea.
4	to ask someone to repeat something	I don't feel like it, actually.
		I'm very grateful to you.
5	to disagree with a suggestion	Oh, go on.
6	to persuade someone	Sorry?
7	when answering someone who thanks you	What would you do?
8	when offering to help	

Exercise 52

34 Telling and asking people to do things

Write eight sensible sentences.

1	Do you feel like	lay the table for me?
2	If I were you,	coming over for a coffee?
3	I'm afraid	having my money back.
4	I insist on	I can't help you just now.
5	I promise	I wouldn't worry about it.
6	It isn't safe,	I'll do better in future.
7	We've decided to	I'm warning you.
8	Would you	take a holiday.

Exercise 53

34 Telling and asking people to do things

Use these words: **Can you ...?/... 'd better ... /... not going to ... / ... decided ... /... really must ... /Shall I ...?/ What about ...?/ Would you like ...?**

Example

Promise to ring Louise tonight.
I'll ring you tonight, Louise.

1. Offer Simon a drink.
2. Offer to hold Alex's glass for a moment.
3. Ask Robert to pass you the salt.
4. Express an intention to join the sports club.
5. Suggest a game of tennis.
6. Refuse to sleep on the floor.
7. Advise Barbara to ring for a doctor.
8. Insist on knowing all the details.

Feelings

Exercise 54

35.1 Being pleased

Write down the five sentences which show that the speaker is pleased.

Good.
Marvellous!
Oh, dear.
Oh, that's wonderful.
Terrific!

That's awful.
That's great.
That's terrible.
What a nuisance!
You're welcome.

Exercise 55

35.2 Likes and dislikes

Write sentences expressing likes and dislikes.

Examples

sunbathing   *(yes, nice)*
Sunbathing is nice.

cowboy films   *(no, not like)*
I don't like cowboy films.

1 cooking   *(yes, enjoy)*
2 walking   *(no, not very interesting)*
3 exams   *(no, hate)*
4 dogs   *(no, can't stand)*
5 discos   *(yes, great)*
6 science fiction   *(yes, like)*
7 chocolate   *(yes, fond of)*
8 swimming   *(yes, love)*
9 cola   *(no, awful)*
10 writing letters   *(no, not like)*

Exercise 56

35.2 Likes and dislikes

There are three groups of sentences in this exercise. Each group contains four sentences expressing how much different people like coffee (A), volley-ball (B) and cats (C). For each group, write the four names in order, beginning with the person who likes coffee etc the most and ending with the person who likes it least.

A   *Kate:*   I don't like coffee.
    Alan: I enjoy a cup of coffee.
    Karen: I can't bear to drink coffee.
    Peter: Coffee is my favourite drink.

B   *Vicky:*   I like volley-ball.
    Michael: I can't stand volley-ball.
    Jane: There's nothing I like better than playing volley-ball.
    Justin: Volley ball isn't very interesting.

C   *Sophie:*   I can't bear cats.
    Darren: I dislike cats.
    Julie: I love cats. They're my favourite animals.
    Nicholas: I'm fond of cats.

Exercise 57

35.2 Likes

Write questions with the word **favourite.**

Example

Colin: What's your favourite animal?
Sarah: The elephant.

1 *Judy:*   …?
   Gary: Red, I think.

2 *Philip:*   …?
   Andrew: Agatha Christie. I love her books.

3 *Paula:*   …?
   Caroline: Basket-ball.

4 *Elizabeth:* …?
   David: I'm not sure. Either history or geography.

▷

5 Mark: ...?
   Sadie: Robert Redford! I think he's great.
6 Sharon: ...?
   James: 'High Noon' is. I've seen it six times.

Exercise 58

35.3 Wishing

What do people say in these situations? Use the words in brackets.

Examples

Alison has never visited Australia, but her greatest wish is to do so. What does she say? *(would love)*
I'd love to visit Australia.

A gang is planning to rob a bank. Their leader's wish is that the plan should succeed. What does he say? *(want)*
I want the plan to succeed.

1 Mrs Vince lost her job recently. It wasn't what she wanted. What does she say? *(wish)*
2 Bob and Alan are having a picnic, but they aren't enjoying it because of all the litter. They wish people would take their litter home. What do they say? *(why can't)*
3 Mrs Andrews is expecting a parcel. Her wish is that the parcel should come. What does she say? *(want)*
4 Fiona has been away from home for three weeks. Her boy-friend Carl hasn't seen her all that time. His greatest wish is to see her again. What does he say? *(dying)*
5 Richard can't get into his flat because he forgot the key when he went out. He's sorry he did that now. What does he say? *(if only)*
6 Andrea thinks she's too fat. She doesn't want to be so fat. What does she say? *(wish)*
7 Mrs Duncan doesn't often go out. But tonight she likes the idea of going out. What does she say to her husband? *(would like)*
8 Nicola likes Peter. She's at a party, but Peter isn't there. She's sorry about that. What does she say? *(if only)*

Exercise 59

35.3 Hoping

The newspaper headlines say what might happen in the future. Say what you hope will happen.

Examples

FIGHTING MAY END SOON
I hope the fighting ends soon.

MILK MAY GET MORE EXPENSIVE
I hope milk doesn't get more expensive.

Feelings

Exercise 60

35.4 Preferences

Ask people which they prefer.

Examples

Tea? Coffee?
Would you rather have tea or coffee?

Go out? Stay in?
Would you rather go out or stay in?

1. Do some more work? Have a rest?
2. Pop music? Classical music?
3. Meat? Fish?
4. Walk? Go on your bike?
5. Read? Watch television?
6. Go shopping? Look round the museum?
7. A hot meal? Just a sandwich?
8. Pay in cash? With a cheque?

Exercise 61

35.4 Preferences

Express a preference using the words in the brackets.

Examples

You like wearing jeans. You don't like wearing trousers so much. *(would rather)*
I'd rather wear jeans than trousers.

You don't like very hot weather. You like cool weather. *(prefer)*
I prefer cool weather to very hot weather.

You like living in a town. You don't like living in the country so much. *(better)*
I like living in a town better than in the country.

1. You like playing tennis. You don't like going swimming so much.
   (would rather)
2. You don't like staying in one place. You like travelling around. *(better)*
3. You don't like cats, but you like dogs. *(would rather)*
4. You like brown bread. You don't like white bread so much. *(prefer)*

5   You don't like running much, but you like gymnastics. *(better)*
6   You like Scotland. You don't like England so much. *(prefer)*
7   You don't like going to a disco very much, but you enjoy going to a party. *(would rather)*
8   You like small shops. You don't like supermarkets. *(prefer)*

Exercise 62

35.5   Showing surprise

Write down the four sentences which show that the speaker is surprised at the news he/she has just heard.

I don't mind.
I don't believe it.
I've no idea.
Is it really?
It isn't, is it?

Yes, it is.
Oh, dear.
OK.
Good heavens.
Not at all.

Exercise 63

35.5   Showing surprise and interest

Tell people what you have heard about them, and show surprise or interest.

Examples

You are surprised to hear that Richard gets up at four o'clock in the morning.
You don't get up at four o'clock in the morning, do you?

You are interested to hear that Carol has found a flat.
You've found a flat, have you?

1   You are surprised to hear that Mr Hurd is ninety years old.
2   You are interested to hear that Tom has bought an old London taxi.
3   You are surprised to hear that Mr Dawson travels a hundred miles to work every day.
4   You are surprised to hear that Paul has got nine sisters.
5   You are interested to hear that Mrs Price is a detective.
6   You are interested to hear that Alison lives in a caravan.
7   You are interested to hear that Helen once hitch-hiked round the world.
8   You are surprised to hear that Mrs Jennings likes punk music.

44 Feelings

Exercise 64

35.6 Regret

Express your regret at what happened. Begin **It's a pity ...** or **I regret ...** .

Examples

You lost the game. *(pity)*
It's a pity I lost the game.

You didn't lock the car. *(regret)*
I regret not having locked the car.

1 You didn't do enough studying. *(regret)*
2 All the glasses got broken. *(pity)*
3 You didn't see Lucy. *(regret)*
4 You didn't book a holiday. *(pity)*
5 You sold all your cassettes. *(regret)*
6 The party wasn't a success. *(pity)*
7 You got angry with Matthew. *(regret)*
8 You called him an idiot. *(regret)*

Exercise 65

35.6 Regret and being pleased

What would you say in these situations? Use **I'm sorry ...** or **I'm glad ...** .

Examples

Simon hasn't been very well. What do you say to him?
I'm sorry you haven't been very well.

You passed your English exam.
I'm glad I passed my English exam.

1 You didn't bring any money with you.
2 You arrived home late at night. You remembered your keys.
3 Anne didn't have time to visit you. What do you say to her?
4 You had to hurry for the train, but you didn't miss it.
5 You saw something interesting, but you didn't have your camera with you.
6 Anthony has been on holiday. His hotel wasn't very nice. What do you say to him?
7 The weather was good. What do you say to Anthony?
8 Anthony had a good time. What do you say to him?

Exercise 66

35.7 Worry

Write the dialogue with the correct expressions.

Rachel: | Is anything wrong, | Claire? |
         | Is something mattering, |
         | Is there trouble, |

Claire: Yes.

Rachel: | What is there? |
         | What's the matter? |
         | What's the worry? |

Claire: I forgot to do my maths homework.

Rachel: | Well, | don't worry. |
         | | it doesn't worry. |
         | | no worrying. |

Mr Grant will let you hand it in tomorrow, won't he?

Claire: | I don't know. | I'm worried about | getting a bad mark. |
         | | It's a matter |
         | | It troubles me |

Rachel: | Oh, | don't mention it. |
         | | exactly. |
         | | it's all right. |

He won't give you a bad mark just because you forgot.

Claire: I didn't really understand what we did in the last lesson.

Rachel: | Well, | it doesn't do. | Ask him to explain it again.
         | | it doesn't mind. |
         | | it doesn't matter. |

Feelings

Look,	it isn't a worry.
	no worrying.
	there's nothing to worry about.

There's no need to get upset over a little thing like that.

Exercise 67

35 Feelings

What might you say in these situations? Write the expressions with the correct numbers.

1 to express regret	Damn!
2 when someone is worried or upset	Good Lord.
3 when you are annoyed	Marvellous!
4 when you are interested	Oh, really?
5 when you are pleased	What a shame.
6 when you are surprised	What's up?

Exercise 68

35 Feelings

Write eight sensible sentences.

1 I can't stand	about the exam.
2 I'm afraid	you wouldn't shout.
3 I'm very fond	I've got some bad news.
4 I'm worried	of my girl-friend.
5 It doesn't matter to me	sit or stand?
6 I wish	the train's on time.
7 Let's hope	this awful weather.
8 Would you rather	what people say.

Right and wrong

Exercise 69

36.1 Approving and disapproving

Rewrite the sentences using **I approve** ... or **I disapprove** ....

Examples

I'm in favour of the idea.
I approve of the idea.

People oughtn't to park their cars here.
I disapprove of people parking their cars here.

1 I'm against experiments on animals.
2 It's a good idea to clean up old buildings.
3 I'm in favour of the new plan.
4 People shouldn't go on strike all the time.
5 I'm pleased the government are keeping down prices.
6 I'm against nuclear weapons.
7 It's wrong to borrow money.
8 It's a good idea for young people to take an interest in politics.

Exercise 70

36.1 + 33.5 Approving, disapproving and opinions

Bob and Helen are arguing about women's rights.

Write the dialogue with the correct expressions.

Bob:	As it seems, I seem It seems to me	this Women's Lib business has gone too far.

▷

Helen: | Oh, | I agree | the Women's Liberation Movement. |
| | I'm in favour of | |
| | I'm pleased | |

Bob: | Well, | I'd feel | it's gone too far. |
| | I say | |
| | I wonder | |

Helen: | I approve | we women are standing up for ourselves at last. |
| I'm glad | |
| I've no idea | |

Yes,	I'm all for it.
	I'm sure.
	quite.

Bob: But why do women just want to be like men?

I disapprove of	women going out to work.
I don't believe	
I'm afraid	

As I'm concerned	a woman's place is in the home.
As I think,	
In my opinion,	

Helen: You're about a hundred years behind the times, Bob. Most women can do a job as well as a man, if not better.

Bob: Well, women are better at housework, of course.

I don't agree	for a man to do housework.
It isn't my opinion	
It's not right	

Helen: | I see | men have had their own way for too long. |
| I think | |
| To my belief, | |

But that's changing now, you know...

Exercise 71

36.2 Blaming someone

Say who was to blame in these situations and what they should or shouldn't have done.

Example

One day Mrs Best didn't shut the garden gate. Her 2-year-old daughter Sharon ran into the road and was knocked down by a van. She was badly hurt. The driver had no time to stop.

It was Mrs Best's fault. She should have shut the garden gate.

1. Simon had a date with Judy last night, but he forgot about it. Judy waited half an hour for him outside the cinema. She was rather angry with him.
2. Stephen was riding home on his bicycle last night when a car hit him and knocked him over as he was riding along. The driver just didn't see Stephen although there were lights on the bike.
3. Paula lost her ticket for the concert last Friday. She explained to the woman at the door what had happened, but the woman refused to let her in.
4. Kevin did very badly in his maths exam. He didn't do any work for the exam. His sister Angela is good at maths and sometimes helps him with it, but she was ill just before Kevin's exam.
5. There was a fire at a dance hall in London last week. A lot of young people were killed. The porter had locked nearly all the doors, and people couldn't get out quickly enough. The manager had told the porter to lock the doors.
6. Mr Hudson painted a bedroom door yesterday, but he didn't tell his wife what he was doing. She hung her coat on the door and got paint all over it. She didn't notice the wet paint on the door.
7. Claire bought an expensive camera, and the next day she dropped it and it broke. She took it back to the shop, but the manager refused to give her a new one.
8. It snowed heavily in the night, but Mr Moxon didn't clear the snow from his path. The postman was walking up to the door at half past nine the next morning when he slipped in the snow and fell down, hurting himself.

50 Right and wrong

Exercise 72

36.4 Apologies

How do you apologize in these situations?

Example

when you forgot about something – *I'm sorry I forgot.*

1. when you can't help someone
2. when you didn't have time to do something
3. when you're late
4. when you couldn't go to a meeting
5. when you didn't tell someone something
6. when you've kept someone waiting

Exercise 73

36 Right and wrong

How might you use the following sentences? Write each of the numbers 1–6 with the correct phrase or sentence.

1 to accept an apology	Can't something be done about it?
2 to approve of something	I'm awfully sorry.
3 to apologize	It doesn't matter.
4 to disapprove of something	It's a good idea.
5 to blame someone	It's wrong to do that.
6 to complain	It's your fault.

Exercise 74

36 Right and wrong

Write six sensible sentences.

1 I approve of	I opened your letter.
2 I blame	I don't think I want to come here again.
3 It isn't right	it doesn't happen again.
4 I'm sorry	people looking after their health.
5 I'm sorry to have to say this, but	the so-called experts.
6 That's all right, as long as	to give pupils so much homework.

General Communication

Exercise 75

32–34 Communication

Birgit, a girl from Germany, is spending some time at an English school. Today she's working in the library. She wants to ask the librarian a question.

Write out in full each sentence that has a word missing. Use these words: **actually, all, excuse, mean, much, right, see, thing, understand.**

Birgit:	___¹ me.
Librarian:	Yes, can I help you?
Birgit:	I don't ___² the sentence here in the front of this dictionary. What does it ___³?
Librarian:	'This book is for reference only.' It means you aren't allowed to borrow it.
Birgit:	But I can take it out of the library if I have a ticket, can't I?
Librarian:	No, ___⁴, you can't. You're only allowed to use it in the library to look up a word. The ___⁵ is so many people need to use it, you see.
Birgit:	I can take it to that table over there, can't I? I can use it anywhere in the library, you mean.
Librarian:	Yes, that's ___⁶.
Birgit:	I ___⁷. Thank you very ___⁸.
Librarian:	That's ___⁹ right.

Exercise 76

34 + 35 Communication

Adrian offers to help Terry move his things into his new flat.

Write the dialogue with the correct expressions.

Terry: I've found a flat at last, Adrian.

Adrian:
All right.	It's a shame	When are you moving in?
Oh, have you?	That's good.	
So you have.	What a nuisance!	

Terry: On Saturday. Mr Dawson's lending me his van.

Adrian: | Do I | give you a hand? Do you need any help? |
| Shall I | |
| Will I | |

Terry: | Oh, | forget it. | I will need some help. |
| | not at all. | |
| | yes, please. | |

Adrian: | What time | are you dying | to start? |
| | are you going | |
| | do you think | |

Terry: | I decide | to start loading the van about nine o'clock. |
| I plan | |
| I think | |

Could you	get to my place around then?
May you	
Should you	

Adrian: | Excuse me. | I'll be there. |
| Instead. | |
| Sure. | |

Terry: | Don't mention it, | Adrian. That's very good of you. |
| I can manage, | |
| Thanks very much, | |

Exercise 77

32–35 Communication

Sarah and Vicky are talking in the coffee bar.

General Communication 53

Write out in full each sentence that has a word missing. Use these words: **intend, like, luck, mean, mind, pity, sorry, sure, thinking, were.**

Sarah: How did you get on in your German exam?
Vicky: I failed it, I'm ___¹ to say.
Sarah: Oh, what a ___². But never ___³. Better ___⁴ next time.
Vicky: There may not be a next time.
Sarah: Oh? What do you ___⁵?
Vicky: I ___⁶ to give up German. I'm not very good at languages.
Sarah: Oh, if I ___⁷ you, I wouldn't give it up. You're ___⁸ to pass next year.
Vicky: I'm ___⁹ of leaving school, actually. I'd ___¹⁰ to get a job.
Sarah: Well, that isn't easy at the moment, you know. And what will your parents say?
Vicky: I don't know. I haven't told them yet.

Exercise 78

32–35 Communication

Karen invites David to a party, but David will be away on holiday.

Complete the conversation by writing a sentence for each part in brackets.

Karen: (*Invite David to a party. Use* **would like.**)
David: Yes, please. When is it?
Karen: On the 22nd, in two weeks' time. Will you be able to come?
David: (*Be unsure. Use the word* **sure.**)
Just a minute, and I'll have a look in my diary.
Karen: (*Express the hope that David can come.*)
David: (*Express regret that you can't come on the 22nd. Use the word* **afraid.**)
I'm going to Scotland with a couple of friends that week. Sorry, I'd forgotten about that.
(*Express your intention to do some walking. Use the word* **plan.**)
Karen: (*Express regret that David will be away that week. Use the word* **pity.**)
But I thought you were going to have a holiday on the canal.
David: Yes, I was. (*Express a preference for spending a holiday on water. Use* **would rather.**)
But I decided it was too expensive.
(*Express a wish for a boat of your own. Use the word* **wish.**)
Karen: Well, never mind. Walking in Scotland sounds OK.
David: Yes, it'll be nice. (*Express a liking for walking, too. Use* **fond of.**)
Karen: (*Express good wishes to David for his holiday. Use the word* **time.**)
David: Thanks.

Exercise 79

35 + 36 Feelings and right and wrong

Find the correct reply.

Example

Angela won the prize. – She did, did she?

1	Angela won the prize.	Good heavens.
2	I'm sorry.	I don't care.
3	I've found the money I lost.	Oh, dear.
4	The Browns have got a pet monkey.	That's all right.
5	The car won't start.	She did, did she?
6	Which one would you like?	That's good.

Exercise 80

35 + 36 Feelings and right and wrong

Which of these expressions belongs to which picture?

I don't believe it. / I'm afraid I have a complaint to make. / I'm sorry. / It was your fault. / Oh, hell! / What's the matter?

Write the expressions with the correct numbers.

Exercise 81

34–36 Communication

Mr Reid is complaining to Mr Banks about the noise. There's a party going on in Mr Banks's flat.

Complete the conversation by writing a sentence for each part in brackets.

Mr Reid: *(Ask Mr Banks to be a bit quieter. Use **would mind**.)*
Mr Banks: We're just having a little party. We aren't disturbing anyone.
Mr Reid: Well, you're disturbing **me**. *(Complain about the noise. Use the word **protest**.)* It's two o'clock in the morning, you know.
Mr Banks: Well, go to bed, then. Just leave us alone.
Mr Reid: How can anyone sleep with all this noise going on? *(Threaten to call the police if he doesn't turn the music down. Begin: **If** ...)*

Mr Banks: Call the police then. *(Refuse to turn the music down for Mr Reid. Use **going to**.)*
Mr Reid: You're keeping me awake. And I have to go to work in the morning.
Mr Banks: Go away, will you? *(Express a strong dislike of people who spoil all the fun. Use the word **bear**.)*

Exercise 82

33–36 Communication

Max and Brian are talking about cigarette smoking.

Complete the conversation by writing a sentence for each part in brackets.

Max: I see the government has put another 5 p on a packet of cigarettes.
Brian: *(Be annoyed. Use the word **no**.)*
Why do we smokers have to pay so much in tax?
Max: *(Advise Brian to stop smoking. Use the words **take** and **advice**.)*
It's not only expensive, it's bad for your health, too.
Brian: Well, that's my business, isn't it? *(Express disapproval that the government makes you pay so much. Use the word **disapprove**.)*
Max: *(Express approval of smokers paying for the cost of their treatment in hospitals. Use **in favour of**.)* *(Express the opinion that cigarettes should be banned anyway. Use the word **opinion**.)*
Brian: *(Express your disapproval of people telling other people what to do. Use the word **against**.)*
Max: *(Express your strong dislike of cigarette smoke. Use the word **stand**.)*
Brian: *(Express your regret that Max doesn't smoke. Use the word **pity**.)*
I won't offer you a cigarette, but you don't mind if I smoke, do you?

Exercise 83

32–36 Communication

Klaus, Peter and Alan are talking about the World Cup.

Write the dialogue with the correct expressions.

Klaus:	Are you going to Do you think of Will you decide to	watch the World Cup game tonight, you two?

Peter: | I'm not. | I don't care | football. |
        | | I hate | |
        | | I mind | |

Alan: | Yes, I'll be watching. I think Scotland are | believed to | win. |
        | | going to | |
        | | supposed to | |

As far as I'm concerned,	they're the best team in Europe just now.
As far as it seems,	
It's absolutely essential	

Klaus: | Exactly. | I don't think they're very good at all. |
         | I disagree. | |
         | I guess. | |

They	shouldn't think to	beat the Germans.
	surely don't	
	won't	

Alan: They beat them two-nil last year.

Klaus: | Two-one, | actually. | And anyway, it was only a friendly game. |
         | | certainly. | |
         | | indeed. | |

Alan: If Jenkins plays for Scotland, they'll win. He's a great player.

The manager was	bound	to leave him out of the team last week.
	right	
	wrong	

Klaus: I think Jenkins is useless.

It was his	blame	Scotland lost against England.
	fault	
	shame	

▷

58   General Communication

Peter: If you two are going to talk about football all the time, I'm going.

> Bye!
> Hi!
> Well done!

Klaus: | Cheerio!
          | Fine!
          | Here's to you!

Alan: | I see, | Peter.
          | See you later,
          | You're welcome,

Exercise 84

32–36   Useful expressions

Look at the expressions below. Find pairs of expressions that have the same use. Match the pairs with the correct use.

Write the numbers with the correct pair of expressions. Put an equals sign between the two expressions.

Example

1   Excuse me. = Pardon me.

Uses	Expressions
1 after sneezing or coughing	Don't mention it.
2 agreeing with an opinion	Enjoy yourself.
3 agreeing with a suggestion	Exactly.
4 answering someone who thanks you	Excuse me.
5 asking someone to repeat something	Good idea.
6 being unsure	Have a good time.
7 good wishes for a holiday	I don't care.
8 having no preference	I don't know.
	It doesn't matter to me.
	I've no idea.
	Not at all.

	Pardon? Pardon me. Quite. Sorry? Yes, why not?

Exercise 85

32–36 Informal expressions

Copy the following table into your exercise book and then complete it. Put neutral expressions (= those which are neither formal nor informal) on the left and informal expressions on the right.

Use these expressions: **Cheerio! / Goodbye! / Hello. / HI. / How are you? / How's life? / I don't get you. / I'm all for it. / I'm in favour of it. / Thanks a lot. / Thank you very much. / What do you mean?**

		neutral	informal
1	approving		
2	being polite when saying hello		
3	not understanding		
4	saying hello		
5	saying goodbye		
6	thanking someone		

Exercise 86

32–36 Formal expressions

Copy the following table into your exercise book and then complete it. Put neutral expressions (= those which are neither formal nor informal) on the left and formal expressions on the right.

Use these expressions: **Allow me. / Certainly. / Good luck. / I'd like to wish you every success. / I'll do that. / I'm sorry. / Please accept my apologies. / Yes, of course. / Yours faithfully. / Yours sincerely.**

		neutral	formal
1	agreeing to a request		
2	finishing a letter		
3	good wishes for success		
4	making an apology		
5	offering to help		

Exercise 87

32.6 + 34.1 Written expressions

Only four of these phrases and sentences are typical of written English. The others are more typical of spoken English.

Write down the four phrases and sentences which are most likely to be written.

Dear Sir,
Excuse me.
Is anything wrong?
It's a pleasure.
How do you do?
Nice to see you.
No parking.
All pupils will attend.
That's right.
With best wishes.

Exercise 88

33–36 Emphatic expressions

Copy the following table into your exercise book and then complete it. Put the emphatic expressions on the right.

Use these expressions: **I can't stand it. / I'd like to see it. / I don't like it. / I'm convinced it is. / I'm dying to see it. / I think it is. / Oh, dear. / Oh, hell! / Thank you. / Thank you very much indeed. / That's good. / That's marvellous.**

	neutral	emphatic
1 being annoyed		
2 being pleased		
3 expressing dislike		
4 expressing a wish		
5 giving an opinion		
6 thanking someone		

Index

Die Ziffern beziehen sich in der Regel auf die Kapitel und Abschnitte (32–36) der *Grammar of Spoken English*. Bezieht sich das Stichwort nur auf eine bestimmte Übung, so wird nur auf diese verwiesen, z. B. *in favour of* E 16 (= Exercise 16).

a/an E 42
what/how about 34.4
advice 34.5
agreeing 33.1,5; 34.4
apologies 36.4
approving 36.1
asking about meaning 33.2
asking for an explanation 33.3
asking for an opinion 33.5
asking for a word 33.2
asking people to do things 34

be going to 34.3
be to 34.1
blaming 36.2

can 34.11
can/could 34.2
compliments 32.8
correcting 33.1
could 34.2, 4

disagreeing 33.1,5; 34.4
disapproving 36.1
dislikes 35.2

emphatic expressions E 88

in favour of E 16
favourite 35.2
feelings 35
finishing a conversation 32
formal/informal E 85, 86

I'm glad E 65
going to 34.3
goodbye 32.5
good wishes 32.7
greetings 32.3,5

had better 34.5
have (= *eat/drink*) 34.11
hello 32.3
hoping 35.3

if 34.6,7
imagining 33.7
imperative 34.1
insisting 34.8
intentions 34.3
interest 35.5
introductions 32.2
invitations 34.12

know 33.4

let me 34.11
let's 34.4
likes 35.2

might 34.3
mind 34.2
must/mustn't 34.1

offers 34.11
opinions 33.5
orders 34.1

permission E 43
persuading 34.9
it's a pity 35.6
being pleased 35.1
predictions 33.6
preferences 35.4
promises 34.10

question tags 35.5

refusing an invitation 34.12
regret 35.6

requests 34.2
right and wrong 36

shall 34.4,11
short answers 33.1
should 34.5
some E 42
sorry 35.6
starting a conversation 32
statements 33
suggestions 34.4
supposing 33.7
be sure to 33.6
being sure and unsure 33.4
surprise 35.5

tags 35.5
telephoning 32.4

telling people to do things 34
thanking 34.13
think 33.4, 34.3
threats 34.7

want 35.3
warnings 34.6
why not 34.4
will 34.7,10,11
will/would 34.2
wishing 35.3
worry 35.7
would 34.2
would like 34.2,11,12
would mind 34.2
would rather 35.4
written expressions E 87